The T...... ...... Experience

Understanding the three levels of glory for Spiritual growth and maturity

Trena, May your life be inspired by the Revelation of these writings! You are purposed for greatness

Dr. Janice Crenshaw

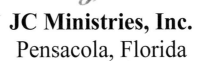

JC Ministries, Inc.

Pensacola, Florida

The Tomb Glory Experience:

Understanding the three levels of glory for spiritual growth and maturity
ISBN 0-9676714-2-6
Copyright 2003

Published by JC Ministries, Inc.
P.O. Box 19053
Pensacola, Fl 32523-9053

Cover design by Stallworth Illustrations
Duncanville, Texas

Dedications

This book is dedicated to the memory of my mother, Mother Myrtis Brown, who went home to be with the Lord in June of 2002. Her divine impartation of wisdom has given me the strength and the courage to know how to persevere through life's challenges.

Acknowledgments

Thanks to my wonderful husband, Bishop John Crenshaw, for your love, support and commitment to prayer that has covered our family for the past twenty-six years. And to my three children, Shakena, Micah and Jasmyn, you are such an inspiration to me. Thank you for your respectful love, support and patience.

Foreword

You are in for a treat that will bless your soul, even as you receive a revelation that will change your life. Each Christian's primary purpose for his or her life should be to glorify our Lord and Savior Jesus Christ. This demands from us a tremendous change from one lifestyle to another, from ungodly to the godly. Unfortunately, too many Christians are avoiding the call in their lives to walk the paths of righteousness. Fear has become our greatest stumbling block. We desire to keep the known, rather than seek and hunger after the unknown.

Jesus, as He was speaking to His disciples after the Last Supper and before the crucifixion, informed the disciples that He was "the way, the truth, and the life" (**St. John 14:7**). Jesus informed them that as they continue to follow Him by allowing their soul to hunger and thirst after Him, He would lead them to a prepared home with Him while they yet lived. A few verses later, He informed them that His Spirit would return and be in them as Comforter, as well as a guide to lead them into all truth. He also informed them that He was the perfect example; that as He was about to die, be buried and resurrect to be with His Father, so we will also die, be buried and resurrect to be with Him. We call it "Born Again".

Dr. Crenshaw's book shows us clearly that this is not an event, but rather a process. Even after our initial born again experience, there will be many more deaths, burials, and resurrections in our life. The way a Christian conquers his enemies is to die to them; for a Christian has been promised everlasting life. We know that when we give up our life, we find it (**St. Matthew 16:25**). Our death is never the end.

More importantly, Dr. Crenshaw blesses us by showing all who read this book that this process is nothing to be dreaded, but to be enjoyed. There can be nothing greater than to be like Jesus. Not only will Heaven rejoice and God get the glory as day by day I become more like my Savior, but my heart will leap for joy as I can walk in His sight; unashamed of my past, because now He gets the glory for the change that has come over me.

This book is not only inspirational and life changing, it is also well written, concise and informative. As you read it over and over again, do not keep it a secret. Give copies to your friends and watch the change that comes over them as they yield to the move of God in their lives.

Bishop Thomas Wesley Weeks, Sr.
New Destiny Fellowship International
Wilmington, Delaware

Preface

How many times have you heard people say...... "I want to be just like Jesus"? It is a statement that is often times used very casually......not realizing the seriousness of the price that has to be paid, which most really don't want to pay. Oh yes, it is very encouraging when we look at the life of Jesus and see the miracles He performed......how He raised the dead, opened blinded eyes and caused the lame to walk. But in all of the miracles that Jesus performed, there was a price to be paid. Personally, I did not realize the seriousness of this price, until I began to be challenged, in life, with experiences that caused me great pain and disappointment. The average expectation of the believer in the "church world" is to be comfortable in an environment that is free from such pain and disappointment. Christians most times live in a "make believe world" thinking that we can purchase God's anointing like we do fast

foods. The charismatic atmosphere in today's church, with the music, the drums,
and the dance is a crutch to many, who fail
to realize that there is a serious price to be
paid to walk in the Christ anointing.

Growing up in a Pentecostal home with
a rich heritage of preachers and pastors, put
me in a very vulnerable position to believe
that anyone who named the name of Christ,
preached the Gospel or laid hands on the
sick, were individuals who had paid the
price to operate in those gifts. As I grew
older, I realized that it was more to it than
being able to preach a sermon, arouse the
crowd, and dance until midnight. When the
music stopped, the dancing was over, and
the lights went out in the church, then
what? Time, age and experience afforded
me a different outlook on life in the church,
as we traditionally know it, and what life in
Christ was really all about. The death, burial and resurrection of Jesus became more
of a revelation to me as never before. I began to see myself going through the death ,
burial and resurrection process, not knowing what in the world was happening to me.
All I knew was that I was sick and tired of

the "status quo" in church. I wanted more from God. I wanted to know Him in the power of His resurrection and in the fellowship of His suffering. Needless to say, that I was desiring to wake up with suffering, have breakfast, lunch and dinner with suffering, and then retire for the evening with suffering. "Suffering" became my best friend. That's what you call fellowship. You can't even fellowship with an individual unless you spend time with them. Please let me clarify what I mean when I speak of suffering. I was naturally blessed. My husband and I had purchased five homes during our twenty-six years of marriage. We drove a jaguar and owned two other vehicles. The Lord had blessed us to purchase a beautiful church at 75% below the market value, that sat on 1.3 acres of land in the heart of the city, with seven members, when we began pastoring thirteen years ago. My suffering had nothing to do with the lack, or the possession of material things. We must be careful about measuring one's relationship with God by material blessings. Additionally, the lack of material blessings does not mean that one is suffering for Christ. It was simply my desire to be like Jesus that plunged me into the death, burial and resurrection process that revealed to me the real meaning of suffering for Christ.

As I've walked through many wilderness experiences in my life, it has taught me that it is more than just a statement to say...... "I want to be like Jesus". It is a statement that means, "Yes Lord" to began the death, burial and resurrection process in your personal relationship with God. Each level of this process is a testing ground, and if you are not careful, you will get stuck in the midst of the process and never be resurrected in the "true" Christ anointing. Just some food for thought.......there will be a resurrection, in spite of how you die. For there is a first and a second resurrection, as written in the Word of God. The second resurrection has no power. Therefore, as a believer, you should strive to not just be resurrected, but to be resurrected in the right spirit...the Christ anointing. Ask God to help you see yourself as you read the revelation that is given in this book. At the conclusion, I pray that you will come to know and understand that submission to the process of death, burial and resurrection, will secure your keys to unlock your destiny.

Table of Contents

Introduction

One day I was driving down the street, feeling rather low in spirit and feeling as though I had absolutely no one to talk to. God had blessed me to have a good husband, who loved God and would give anything to support me in whatever I set out to do. He has never tried to hinder me from doing the work of God, and has always been supportive in all of my life's endeavors. Therefore, I was fortunate and grateful to God for that simple fact. I knew I could always depend on Godly counsel from my mother, who was a woman of wisdom, and was dedicated to prayer. I always knew that whatever I undertook to do, and where ever I went, she would always be praying for me. Even in my ministerial travel, I knew that each time I boarded a plane, my mother would be praying until the day I walked back into the house. But even in knowing all of this, and having the support of a good husband and a praying mother, I believe I was in a place where God was trying to show me something in the spirit. I believe He was allowing me to experience moments of loneliness, to help me to understand where I was in my spiritual walk with Him. I had come to a place, in ministry, where it was very difficult for me to trust, particularly those in the church. I had allowed the weaknesses of others to out weigh what God was trying to birth within me. I had failed to realize that <u>each experience was allowed by God to help me recognize the weaknesses within myself.</u> He was trying to walk me through the necessary process to become a true "Son of God". Many times we don't realize what is in us, until we come "face to face" with the enemy of our own soul. Remember, when God spoke in Exodus 23:20 and told the children of Israel that the angel of the Lord was going to lead them in unto the Amorites, the Hivites the Jebusites, the Hittites, the Perizzites, and the Canaanites to possess their blessed land. That means that the Children of Israel had to face their enemy to get to their land of promise. You too, must come face to face with your own enemy before you walk into your place of promise. You will be tested with what God is trying to get out of you, to purify you for the next level in Him. You may be asking God..... "Why do I have to keep facing this Amorite spirit?" Historically, the Amorites were militant people. They had a fighting spirit. Many times God will allow you to keep facing individuals who are always trying to pick a fight, because He wants to make sure all the fight is out of you. He wants to make sure that you can face that spirit, without submiting to the ways of the flesh.

So, here I was at a very unusual place in my spiritual walk with God. I was not able to recognize that all I had gone through, and that which I was presently experiencing was symbolic to the life of Jesus being made manifest in my mortal flesh.

Always bearing about in the body the dying of the Lord Jesus, that the life also of Jesus might be made manifest in our body. For we which live are always delivered unto death for Jesus sake, that the life also of Jesus might be made manifest in our mortal flesh. (II Corinthians 4:10-11)

Therefore, instead of allowing God to propel me to the next level, I was stuck in the midst of the process, focusing on the weaknesses in others and not focusing on what God was trying to birth in me through this process. I was truly being born again.

Birthing is a process. Usually a baby is not born until the onset of labor, with the breaking of the water and the bloody show. I said, *usually* ....because in some cases the doctor may induce labor, and/ or puncture the birthing sack to break the water, prior to actual birth. The birthing process begins with labor, and is complete at the passing of the after birth (placenta). The Lord began to speak to me and say, "Your wilderness experience is your birthing canal". In a later chapter, I will explain exactly what God revealed to me about this statement. God said to me, "You must go through this process to birth all I have for you". So as I drove down the street thinking to myself, God would not allow me to think of one person to call, who could help me understand where I was at that time in my spiritual walk. Being a preacher of the Gospel for almost twenty-five years and pastoring along with my husband for more than twelve years, people have a tendency to think that you have a license not to hurt, and you never need spiritual counsel. But this was a time when God Himself, wanted to be my spiritual counselor.

Suddenly, as I was driving and listening to Gospel music, in my car, the voice of the Lord spoke to me in a still soft voice, and said, *"My child come out of the tomb".* I paused for a moment and said to myself, *"Lord, what did you say?"* He said it again, *"My child come out of the tomb".* This was the beginning of a revelatory understanding that I could have never gotten from any other person, other than God Himself. Therefore, He put me in a spiritual place to experience the loneliness of a dark tomb......like the one where Jesus was laid, when He gave His life for mankind. This is where it all began. From that point, God took me back to how He died on the cross, and was put on public display for the sins of this world. God allowed me to see that I was at a place where I had gone through the process of public display and survived the pain of public opinion.

I remember when I published one of my first books, _Spiritual Ejaculation: The Final Hours of Great Deception_, I went through great persecution, much of which came from the church. It took me three years to obey God in writing this book, after being strongly encouraged by a mother in the Church of God in Christ, who heard me teach this revelation at a women's retreat. I knew that when I wrote the book, it would bring about much controversy, but I also knew that God had given me a revelation that would make the powers of the enemy take notice, in that someone was bold enough to deal with the "real deal". I took a chance for God and obeyed Him, and as a result, many people were delivered and blessed. I remember a few months after the book had been published, Dr. Wanda Turner, had gotten a hold to one of my books. After reading it, she picked up the phone, called my office and requested twenty books to be overnighted to her immediately that day. She wanted the books for several Pastors who were to be in Los Angeles for a conference on the next day. I immediately had my office overnight the books.....and about two weeks later, I received a letter from Dr. Turner, stating that because of the quick response to her request, a marriage was saved. All Glory is due to God for His divine direction in simply obeying Him. I could speak to many other testimonies that account to my obedience to God in revealing this controversial revelation........ that dealt with very sensitive areas in the Body of Christ that most would dare not touch, because of the fear of persecution and lack of support from colleagues in the Gospel. I came to realize that there are people, including Spirit-filled believers, who are really hungry for the truth and desire real answers to real problems in life. But there is a price to be paid when you walk in total obedience to God. Even Jesus felt the agony in His flesh in total obedience to the Will of the Father.

Oh Father, if it be possible, let this cup pass from me: nevertheless not as I will, but as thou wilt. **(St. Matthew 26:39)**

You must go through the ugliness of the cross, and the loneliness of a tomb to be resurrected in the Christ Anointing. On the cross, you die to public opinion and the traditions of men. You enter into a third dimension of His Glory to receive revelation that is not common to the "status quo" of the traditional church. From the cross, you are transported to the place of the tomb. It was here that I began to feel lonely and all alone, not realizing that there was a new beginning and a fresh anointing awaiting me outside of the tomb. I had gotten stuck in the tomb, trying to discover destiny in a dead environment, inside of dead relationships.

God began to speak to me about the three levels of glory relative to my personal growth in Him.

Death
The First Level of Glory is the cross.

Burial
The Second Level of Glory is the tomb.

Resurrection
The Third level of Glory is the resurrection.
But we all, with open face beholding

*as in a glass the glory of the Lord,
are changed into the same image
from glory to glory, even as by the
Spirit of the Lord.* **(II Corinthians 3:18)**

Stop right now and consider if you have even begun the process, or are you just enjoying the charismatic flow of being in an atmosphere of "status quo" church, having the form of godliness, but denying His power? Are you hiding out in a cave somewhere trying to keep yourself from being thrown into the death, burial, and resurrection process, because of fear, pride and lack of submission to the divine Will of God for your life?

Get ready to be changed, and to never be the same again. I speak prophetically that many of you, as you read this book, are going to immediately see where you are, understand where you've been, and accept the challenge to go where you've already been sent.

Chapter One
The Process Begins

How precious it is to grow up in a home where there is real love, and to have a mother who would almost give her life to make sure her children survived. I was blessed to have that kind of a mother, who worked very hard to take care of my sister and I, after my father passed away when I was very young. In June of 2002, my mother went home to be with the Lord. The things I miss the most, are her words of wisdom and her dedication to prayer. I don't remember very much about my father, only that he was an Army Veteran, who was a Private Investigator that owned a restaurant in Mobile, Alabama called the "Street Car". All I can really remember is my mother picking me up in her arms, at my father's funeral, to view his body in the coffin, the blowing of the trumpet, and the folding of the American flag at the grave side.

I will never forget, several years ago, I was listening to the radio in Pensacola and there was a special program being aired, in Mobile, where people were asked to call in and talk about precious memories of the past. As I listened, someone called in and mentioned the name Fred Brown and the *Street Car*, which is the restaurant my father owned. I said to myself, "That's my father they're talking about". Almost twenty-five years after my father's death, the impact he had made on his community was still fresh in the minds of people. That seemingly insignificant experience, made a lasting impact upon my life. I immediately began to ask myself...how many times have I left long lasting impressions upon the minds of people, not because of personal accomplishments, but because of total obedience to God. I was challenged to began to assess my personal relationship with God. I made a decision to give as much energy to finding out what my true purpose was in life, as I had given to accomplishing other personal goals. Every experience, from that moment on, was orchestrated by God. I began to be challenged in every area of my life. The Lord began to reveal to me three personal keys to fulfilling His divine Will for my life.

- **remain humble to receive Godly counsel and instruction**

- **maintain pure motive in all that you do**

- **be willing to plant seeds in another's ministry**

Each step is a prerequisite to the other. You can't plant seeds into another's ministry, if your motives are not pure and you are not *in what you are doing for the right reasons;* and if your motives are not pure in what you are doing, then you will not receive Godly council or instruction from anyone.

My life began to be challenged in each of these areas. In 1980, God blessed my husband and I with our first home, which we purchased at 25% of its value. We had 75% equity in the home, at the time of purchase. We immediately refinanced our home, and gave the money to the church to purchase a sanctuary. We gave away all but one of the five cars we personally owned, at the time, to those in need; purchased our pastor a Cadillac, and offered him one of the three houses we owned. God would speak to me about planting seeds into certain ministries, for a period of time, until He released me. I could give countless other testimonies on this subject, but the point I am trying to make is that God will challenge you to be in total obedience and submission to His will.

The Lord began to deal with me in a very peculiar way, through divine revelation of His Word, on subjects that would provoke thought in very sensitive areas of peoples' lives, especially the lives of Spirit-filled believers. My desire to be totally obedient to God, plunged me into the birthing canal of the wilderness experience. This wilderness experience began at the cross, after true repentance of turning away from doing things my way to accept God's way.

The first level of glory is the cross

As I studied the Word, I began to ask God questions about everything. Words in the scripture would just jump out at me. I began studying..... not for a message, but to have a message at all times. I was not moved by "status quo" church. I wanted more from God. I wanted to experience His glory. Well, needless to say, I had no idea what I was asking for, or what I was about to experience. I really was not ready for the first level of glory, which God revealed to me was the cross. This is a very ugly place in the growth process. Everyone is looking at you when you are on the cross. You are truly on public display, or should I say, "you are the talk of the town". The pain and the agony you feel are seen by the masses. The cross is a place where you must strive to stay focused on your purpose and destiny. For there will be times when you'll be tempted to remove yourself from the cross. There will even be those around you, who will try to get you to come down, like they did Jesus.

> *Thou that destroyest the temple, and buildest it in three days, save thyself. If thou be the Son of God, come down from the cross.*
> **(St. Matthew 27:31)**

How many times has someone said to you, "If I were you, I would not take all that"? Many times you will find yourself in a situation where you are being encouraged, even by believers who are weak, to disobey God and remove yourself from the very situation that will propel you into divine destiny. It is at the cross where you must make a decision to give up your Will, as Jesus gave up the ghost. When you make the decision to give your life totally over to the Will of God in the spirit of obedience, it is at that point that you die to the Will of the flesh. You are now ready to enter into the second level of glory, which is the "tomb". This is the level I want to give much attention to, because this is the level that I found myself getting stuck for some length of time. First of all, I had not even recognized that I was experiencing the **first level of glory**, until God revealed to me that I had entered into the second.

Take a moment right now, and ask yourself are you still moved by the opinions of men, when it comes to being totally obedient to God. Are you trying to keep yourself from being placed on public display because of pride, when you know God has spoken to you? That means you will go to any extent to attempt to protect yourself from negative public opinion, even if it means lying or cheating against another to protect your own interest? These are issues that will hinder and halt your growth process in the Lord. Yes, **the cross does bring about public humiliation**, and what you are experiencing is all out in the open. But God is challenging you to stay on the cross and die to the Will of the flesh. For many believers are attempting to be resurrected without going through the death of the cross, and believe it or not, many are being resurrected in an anointing that is not of Christ. Let me provoke some thought......... "where do you think false prophets come from?" Many have gotten down off the cross before time, and have attempted to go into the tomb, without the flesh being dead. And when they got into the tomb, they received an impartation from the underworld, because they had no power to take authority over the spirits of the underworld. Remember, when Jesus was laid in the tomb, He did not stay there. He went into the lower parts of the earth and led captivity captive. <u>A live man can't live in a tomb</u>, <u>and a live man can't conquer the powers of darkness until he gives up the ghost</u>...that means he must die to his own Will. God is challenging you to stay on the cross and prepare yourself for the next level of glory....... "the tomb".

The second level of glory is the tomb

On that beautiful sunny day, as I was riding down the street feeling as though my whole world had come to a stop, I finally realized that what I had been experiencing was severe growing pains of the death, burial and resurrection process. I was actually living the scriptures that Paul spoke about in II Corinthians the 4th chapter.......... "the life of Jesus being made manifest in our mortal flesh". The Lord began to rehearse all that I had gone through, and helped me to understand that I was stuck in the tomb and was refusing to come out. Let me take a moment and explain to you how serious this place is in the spirit. Remember, when you are on the cross everyone sees your pain and what you are going through. But when you decided to die to the Will of the flesh, you were then removed from the cross and shoved into the tomb. This is a very dark and lonely place, because the people who saw you on display are no longer communicating with you, because they think it is all over for you. As a matter of fact, you keep trying to communicate with the ones who have counted you for dead, and you wonder why you get no response. Consider........ have you ever seen a sane individual talk to a dead man, looking to get a response? So why are you trying to get responses from those who are still alive to the Will of the flesh, who cannot comprehend where you are in God?

The tomb was a very significant challenge for me, because I came to realize that even though I felt I had passed the test of public display, and did not remove myself from the ugliness of the cross, I was now in a place where I had to deal with issues on another level. When you are on the cross, people see the tears streaming down your cheeks like drops of blood, and the sweat settling on your face, like steady streams of water. But when you are removed from the cross, they cannot see the many nights you cry, and you travail before God because you are dealing with warfare on a different level. Actually the public view is that, it's all over for you. Your name is no more in lights for the public to see. You are a forgotten trophy with no memory of your place in society . There is no more mention of your ministry. Every now and then, people seem to wonder what in the world has happened to you. What the public does not realize is that you have been privately transported to another level of glory..... *"the tomb"*. God has personally said, "Well done, you have passed the test of the cross and are now qualified to deal with the powers of darkness". This is a place where you have to be very careful, not to find yourself getting stuck and refusing to move on through the tomb, in preparation for a resurrection. Because it is very easy to have a private pity party that seems to last forever.

I want to take some time to explain to you some of the spirits that can attempt to attach themselves to you, as you go through this level of growth. First of all, as I've said before, symbolically, the tomb is a dark and lonely place. Therefore, you must be warned not to allow the spirits that operate in darkness to overtake you while you experience this level of growth. Because you are no longer a public figure in the minds of the people, they are convinced that you are no longer a threat to them in the natural realm. When Jesus hung his head and died, the enemy actually thought he had won the battle until Jesus showed up in hell. What the enemy does not realize is that you have been shoved into the tomb to gain more power and authority over him .....more power than you had while you were hanging on the cross, in the public's view.

The Lord had to really deal with me on this level, because I was really having difficulty coming through this difficult place. It was like I wanted to make my home in the tomb. Until one day the Lord spoke to me and said... *"My child come out of the tomb"*. This utterance from the mouth of God was so powerful that it changed my entire life. I had spent many sleepless and restless nights weeping and crying before God, because I needed victory over the inner pain that could not be seen by men. I came to realize that the tomb was a spiritual place to conquer spirits on another level. **This level of glory is the place where intercession is birthed in your life.** You can't talk about what you are going through, because it cannot be explained in the natural realm. This is the place where God ministers to you. It is a place where you are hungry for rhema messages and prophetic words that come from the third dimension of His glory. Later on in the book, I will reveal to you the revelation God gave me relative to the death, burial and resurrection process, the wilderness experience, and the Tabernacle of Moses.

As God continued to minister to me, in my car about the tomb, I found myself weeping before God and saying to Him, *"Lord now I understand"*. I had gotten stuck in the midst of the tomb glory experience, because I was trying to discover destiny and fulfill purpose inside of the tomb. I was trying to build relationships, and find fellowship in a place where my purpose for being there was not to build relationships and find fellowship. It was a place to heal the inner pain and hurts that could not be seen to the public eye. It was a place for the birthing of prayer and intercession. The problem was that I was so ignorant to this level of growth that I was refusing to go any further. Therefore, I found myself knocking on tomb stones, and to my ignorant surprise, I would get no answer. I suddenly realized that I was spiritually alive in the tomb, and my purpose for being there was to discover treasures that were hidden in this dark place. God was preparing me for resurrection to another level in Him that I was not ready to accept.

And I will give thee the treasures of darkness, and hidden riches in secret places, that thou mayest know that I, the Lord, which call thee by thy name, am the God of Israel.
Isaiah 45:3

I will never forget as God was bringing me through this rough place in my life, Prophetess Juanita Bynum was scheduled to have her second Women Weapons of Power Conference in Pensacola, in August of 2001. I had missed the first conference in August of 2000, but I had made a commitment to myself that I was going to make sure that I attend the conference in 2001. I will never forget the first night of the conference. The Spirit of the Lord was so intense that Prophetess Bynum didn't even preach, but she began to minister into the lives of the people. This was the night that God reconfirmed to me the place, in Him, that He had called me to. When Prophetess Bynum called me out, she began to speak into my life about a supernatural level, and a supernatural realm in God. This supernatural realm is a place beyond the veil ....a place of resurrection to a new identity in

Christ. Now granted I already knew this, but it was such a lonely place, until I was spending more time allowing my spirit to be controlled by the loneliness that I could not see where I was headed. But these simple prophetic words sealed a revelatory understanding of where I was in my spiritual growth in God. The Lord had personally transported me to this place of the tomb, to conquer spirits on another level to be set free from *self*, and as a result, I would obtain the power to release others from captivity. → me

In the book of II Kings, the anointing upon Elisha was so powerful that even after his death, the anointing in his bones resurrected a dead man.

> *And it came to pass, as they were burying a man, that, behold, they spied a band of men; and they cast the man into the sepulcher of Elisha; and when the man was let down, and touched the bones of Elisha, he revived, and stood up on his feet.* **II Kings 13:21.**

I believe God is saying something very prophetic here.....that while you're in the tomb, He is perfecting your grave situation for a resurrection. And in order for God to do that, He has to leave you in a grave situation for a space of time for you to discover the mysteries that are locked up in the tomb. Notice, in the story of Elisha, the dead man hit the bones of Elisha and was resurrected, not his flesh. There was no flesh found in the grave of Elisha. Therefore, he had to have been there for some period of time for his flesh to have returned back to the dust. So it is prophetically. God wants us to be able to minister to others while we are in the tomb, not by way of the flesh, but by His anointing. The same power and authority that was given to Jesus in the tomb, God wants to give it to you.

Wherefore, he saith, when he ascended up on high, he led captivity captive , and gave gifts unto men. Now that he ascended, what is it but that he also ascended first into the lower parts of the earth? He that descended is the same also that ascended up far above the heavens, that he might fill all things. **Ephesians 4:8-10**

So, here I was trying to live out the fulfillment of my destiny in the tomb. God said to me, "this is why you are feeling lonely and alone". "You were sent here to take care of business, not to be overtaken by the powers of darkness that rule in this realm", spirits such as depression, oppression, fear, doubt, unbelief, and even death. If you continue to try and live in the tomb, being dead to the flesh, but alive in the spirit, you will eventually die in the spirit. I had to accept the call of God to come out of the tomb. It was time for a resurrection. It was time to go to another level in God. God said to me, "If you would come out of the tomb, I will receive you on another level of my glory".....the level that Paul longed to experience, when he said, "I want to know Him in the power of His resurrection and in the fellowship of His sufferings".

Assess where you are in your walk with the Lord. Are you feeling spiritually alone, as if there is no one else who's experiencing what you are feeling? Well, Jesus may be calling you forth out of the tomb to another level in Him. Stop knocking on tomb stones, and having fellowship in a place where you have been called out of. There is another level awaiting you in His presence.

Chapter Two
The Revelation Of The Birthing Canal

As the Lord continued to deal with me about my personal relationship with him, these prophetic words began to ring in my spirit. I could hear the Lord saying...... "Your wilderness is your spiritual birthing canal". I began to meditate on this prophetic utterance. The more I meditated on this word, the more God would give me divine revelation. We must understand that every scripture in the Word of God has practical implications for our daily lives. I begin to see how the wilderness experience is very symbolic to natural birth; and natural birth is very symbolic to spiritual birth; and spiritual growth is very symbolic to the Tabernacle of Moses. This will take a little effort for me to explain, so I suggest you stop right here and pray. Ask the Lord to help you receive this revelation on a spiritual level.

Your wilderness experience is your birthing canal

The children of Israel wondered through the wilderness for forty years, because of their disobedience. Jesus, being filled with the Holy Ghost in St. Matthew the 4th chapter, was led by the spirit into the wilderness to fast for forty days and forty nights, to be tempted of the devil. Jesus knew specifically why He had to go to the wilderness, because He knew that Satan had set up his residence there. Remember, the children of Israel chose to go through the wilderness murmuring and complaining against Moses, instead of praising and worshiping God for setting them free from bondage. They had the authority to create an atmosphere, in the wilderness, that reverenced the Spirit of the Almighty God, but they chose to rebel and even worship idol gods. Their disobedience not only extended the time that it took for them to get to the promise land, but from a spiritual perspective, their disobedience created another level of spiritual warfare for the believer who must also go through the wilderness experience to possess the promise. <u>Show me a believer who has never had a wilderness experience, and I will show you an individual who has never known God.</u> The length of time it takes one to go through this process is dependent upon your obedience to God. God can, and will redeem time for you, in the midst of your wilderness experiences. That is exactly what I believe God did when Jesus went into the wilderness to fast forty days and forty nights. My first question is, "why forty"? Why not just three days or seven days? <u>I firmly believe that Jesus went into the wilderness to fast forty days, to fix forty years worth of mess, that had been created by the Children of Israel in the wilderness.</u> God can do the same for you. He can fix twenty years worth of mess in your life, in twenty minutes; ten years worth of mess, in ten minutes---- if you choose to obey Him.

God began to really deal with me about this revelation, relative to natural birth, the wilderness, and the Tabernacle of Moses, and how this revelation relates to our spiritual growth in the Lord. It gave me clarity about every level of my spiritual growth.   I want to share this revelation with you and pray that God will show you yourself, in this process, as He has shown me.   Consider these factors, which I will attempt to explain in the diagram on the next page. You be the judge and assess whether you see any symbolism.

- **There are 38-42 weeks in the natural birth process, which is an average   of 40 weeks.**

  The children of Israel wondered in the wilderness for 40 years.

  Jesus went into the wilderness and fasted 40 days & forty nights.

- **There are three trimesters in natural birth.**

  There are three sections in the Tabernacle of Moses.

  Man has a three-fold nature (body, soul, spirit)

The Lord revealed to me how all of these factors relate to the death, burial and resurrection process of spiritual growth and maturity. Please stop here and take a few minutes and study this diagram on the next page. If you don't, you may not thoroughly understand some of the things that will be discussed in this chapter.

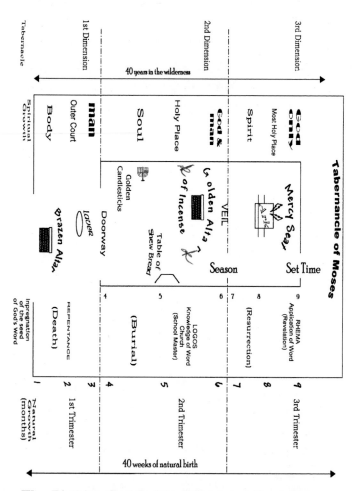

The Birthing Canal of the Wilderness Experience
You may order enlarged copies of this diagram for
teaching, by logging onto www.drjanicecrenshaw.com

As we study the Tabernacle of Moses, we know that it has three dimensions, or three compartments. The Outer Court is the first dimension, symbolic to the first trimester of pregnancy (one to three months), where repentance takes place at the brazen altar. This is the place where you initially hear the Word and you are impregnated with a Word from God, just like when a woman is initially impregnated with a seed from a man. This seed has to be properly nourished, both spiritually and naturally. The Holy Place is the second dimension, symbolic to the second trimester of pregnancy (four to six months), where you obtain knowledge of God's Word from the table of shew bread, which is delivered by the messengers (angels) of the seven churches. Naturally, the second trimester is critical to the growth and development of the child. If the mother is not properly nourished, she could possibly threaten a miscarriage. And if you are not properly nourished with the proper diet, at this level of your spiritual growth, you can miscarriage your destiny and the seed of Gods' Word in you. Now, we know that God was not pleased with all of the seven churches, which are represented by the seven golden candlesticks, in the second dimension, or the Holy Place. Therefore, it is safe to say that we can sometimes be fed the wrong spiritual diet, even from the pulpit. As I studied this revelation, it gave me clarity on how easy it is to get stuck in the second dimension simply having church. We have a lot of knowledge of the Word, but there is little application. <u>In the third dimension, beyond the veil, we apply what we have learned in the second</u>. Many believers get stuck in the midst of the wilderness experience and miscarriage their destiny before it is birthed, in the third dimension, symbolic to the third trimester of pregnancy (seven to nine months). You can only find your true purpose and destiny, in the presence of God, which is beyond the veil. If you never take the time to commune with God, in the third dimension, you will never come to know who you were really destined to be in the mind of God. Before God made you, He had you in His mind. Remember, Jeremiah whom God said, "before you were formed in our mother's belly I knew you and ordained you to be a prophet" **(Jeremiah 1:4)**. But

Jeremiah had to first be born into the earth realm and go through the process of the spiritual birth canal to discover who he had been called to be. It is very clear to me that Jeremiah went through a period of the wilderness, when he said that he was not going to preach again. But because he was destined by God to be a Prophet, he willed himself to respond to the fire he talked about being shut up in his bones. I believe Jeremiah had a choice. You too have a choice as to whether you will go to the next level in God.

Please hear this prophetically, "don't get stuck in the second dimension just having church and miscarriage your destiny in the sixth month." Notice on the diagram, the sixth month was right before the seventh month, which was the entrance into the third dimension, beyond the veil. Now let's consider this from a natural perspective. Most of us know that if a baby is born before the sixth month, it has little chance of survival, unless God prevails. But if the mother carries the child until the seventh month, there may be some complications, but the baby has a better chance of survival, because all of the major organs have developed. So it is spiritually. You can end up losing your seed in the sixth month of your spiritual growth, because you refuse to move past the second dimension into the third. You hear the Word, but you never move past that point to go into the third dimension, beyond the veil, to apply what you have heard in the second dimension.

I have often wondered why the Lord sent an angel down to minister to Mary in the sixth month.

> *And in the sixth month the angel Gabriel was sent from God unto a city of Galilee named Nazareth, to a virgin espoused to a man named Joseph, of the house of David, and the virgin's name was Mary.*
> **St. Luke 1:26-27**

Let me stop here and say how important it is for you to search out the heart and the mind of God. It is okay to ask God ... "Why?" Many times He will answer you with divine revelation that certainly would not have been given, if you had not inquired. So I asked God..... "Why the sixth month?" In St. Luke chapter one, Zechariah went into the temple after the order of the priest to offer up incense .... and while he was praying, the angel of the Lord told Zechariah that Elisabeth was going to have a child, and his name would be called John. We know that the altar of incense, in the Holy Place, represents prayer. Notice on the diagram where the altar of incense is located, relative to natural birth. It is the sixth month. When I read this, my mind immediately went to the revelation that God gave to Prophetess Bynum about praying from the third dimension. One could possibly argue if indeed Zechariah was truly praying from the third dimension. He was certainly right at the point of the ripping of the veil, but it would seem that Zechariah somewhat fail short. The Lord shut his mouth, because he did not believe the revelation that was being revealed to him from the third dimension (beyond the veil), while he was praying at the altar of incense (second dimension). The message the angel delivered to Zechariah was truly a message from be-

[handwritten margin notes: THE MOST → HOLY PLACE "RHEMA" SET TIME]

29

yond the veil, because it did not add up to the natural order of things in the earth realm. Elisabeth was barren and well stricken in age, but the word was... "She would have a son by the name of John". How many times have we prayed in the second dimension, at the altar of incense, and have gotten stuck, and never enter in, beyond the veil, to receive the promises of God? Oh yes, we pray for hours, but sometimes we don't believe what we are praying for. That was Zechariahs' problem. I would argue to say that Zechariah was a second dimension prayer.

And it came to pass, that while he executed the priest's office before God in the order of his course, according to the custom of the priest's office, his lot was to burn incense when he went into the temple of the Lord. And the whole multitude were praying without at the time of incense. And there appearing unto him an angel of the Lord standing on the right side of the altar of incense. And when Zechariah saw him, he was troubled, and fear fell upon him. But the angel said unto him, fear not Zechariah: for thy prayer is heard: and thy

wife Elizabeth Shall bear thee a son, and thou shalt call his name John.
St. Luke 1:8-13

And Zechariah said unto the angel, whereby shall I know this? For I am an old man, and my wife well stricken in years. And the angel answering said unto him, I am Gabriel, that stand in the presence of God; and am sent to speak unto thee, and shew thee these glad tidings. And, behold thou shalt be dumb, and not able to speak, until the day that these things shall be performed, because thou believeth not my words, which shall be fulfilled in their season. **St. Luke 1:18-20**

Notice in **St. Luke 1:20**, the scripture said that the words would be fulfilled in "their" season. "Their" is a possessive pronoun....which means that every prophetic Word, from beyond the veil, has a season. Therefore, you cannot walk into your season of destiny, unless you accept the Word, from beyond the veil, that has your season locked up in it. That's why you cannot believe and receive every prophecy, because every prophecy does not come from the third dimension. Third dimension prophecies speak to the birthing of your divine destiny, in a place beyond the veil in the very presence of God. This is the place where God has destined you to be, even before you were born. Just like he destined Jeremiah to be a prophet before he was formed in his mother's womb. Prophecies from the second dimension are mixed with part truth and part error. It has accurate information, mixed with a little inaccurate information, that will cause you to abort your destiny. I will never forget, some time ago, I was given a prophecy that was very accurate...... that there was a call of God upon my life for Africa. I will speak to this in more detail, in the next chapter. Well, I knew this was an accurate word, because I had experienced over fifteen years of dreams, visions and multiple prophecies about ministering in this country. But the prophecy had enough inaccurate information, mixed with this profound truth, that if I had received it in my heart, it could have caused us to shut the doors of our church, and miss the perfect Will of God. As a result, we would have aborted walking in an overflow of blessings that has put us in a position to be thousands of dollars out of debt. We would have missed receiving a manufactured home that was given to the church, by someone who was just thumbing through the yellow pages of the phone book. And most importantly, we would have aborted the prophetic and apostolic break through that we are now experiencing in the ministry of our local church. I could speak to many more blessing we would have missed, but I think you get the point. That's why so many people are messed up today, including saints. They have depended upon the spiritual gifts of others to define their personal destiny and relationship with God. Because of this, many have married the wrong person, moved to the wrong city, and purchased a life style of debt. They are totally out of the Will of God. You must spend time with God to know him for yourself.

When you enter into His presence, beyond the veil, you will automatically know if any prophetic word being given to you is coming from the third dimension. But how many church going believers are really ready to receive messages from beyond the veil. Third dimension messages don't add up to the normal, traditional, "status quo" of church. Third dimension messages are not compatible to the natural order of things. Usually they make you uncomfortable in your flesh, because in the third dimension, there is no flesh. There's God only. We can be a little more comfortable in the second dimension having church, because in the second dimension there's "God and Man". That's why God found displeasure in some of the seven churches of Asia, which are represented by the seven golden candlesticks in the Holy Place (the second dimension), because flesh was being mixed with the things of God.

Zechariahs' prayers were mixed with unbelief. But his unbelief did not stop God from bringing to pass the prophetic Word that was spoken about the birth of John. Prophetic words from the third dimension cannot be stopped, when one's faith has been released to receive it. Even when it looks dead, it's still alive; and if it dies, it must be resurrected. For when Jesus died, the veil in the tabernacle was ripped from top to bottom, and He entered in beyond the veil to obtain eternal redemption for us. The resurrection anointing rests beyond the veil.

Jesus, when he had cried again with a loud voice, yielded up the ghost. And, behold the veil of the temple was rent in twain from the top to the bottom; and the earth did quake and the rocks rent. **St. Matthew 27:50-51**

But Christ being come an high priest of good things to come, by a greater and more perfect tabernacle, not made with hands, that is to say, not of this building; neither by the blood of goats and calves , but by his own blood he entered in once into the holy place, having obtained eternal redemption for us. **Hebrews 9:11-12**

Remember in the book of II Kings, the 4th chapter, when the prophet Elisha spoke a word to the Shunemite woman, he spoke about her season........a time when she would bare a son. Now once again, this was a third dimension word, that did not add up to the natural order of things in the earth realm. Her husband was old, and she did not expect to ever conceive a child. But notice after the child was born, the child died. But because this prophetic word came from the third dimension, which had her season of destiny locked up in it, the child had to be resurrected.

And he said, about this season, according to the time of life, thou shalt embrace a son. And he said, nay, my Lord, thou man of God, do not lie unto thine handmaid. And the woman conceived, and bare a son at that season that Elisha had said unto her, according to the time of life.

And when the child was grown, it fell on a day, that he want out to his father to the reapers. And he said unto his father , my head. And he said to a lad, carry him to his mother. And when he had brought to his mother he sat on her knees til noon, and then died. **II Kings 4:16-20**

And when Elisha was come into the house, behold, the child was dead, and laid upon his bed. He went therefore, and shut the door upon them twain, and prayed unto the Lord. And he went up and laid upon the child, and put his mouth upon his mouth, and his eyes upon his eyes, and his hands upon his hands; and he stretched himself upon the child; and the flesh of the child waxed warm. Then he returned, and walked in the house to and fro; and went up and stretched himself upon him; and the child sneezed seven times, and the child's eyes opened. **II Kings 4:32-35**

Let me encourage you right now. Any Word that comes from the throne room of God, from beyond the veil, has been signed, sealed and ready to be delivered by God, to you, by your obedience and your faith in Him. It's nothing the enemy can do about it. It may look like you're losing, but you are already a winner. It may look like you're going under, but you are about to cross over. It may look like you're finished, but you have just begun.

Unlike Zechariah, Mary, the mother of Jesus, received a third dimension word that she would bring forth a son, and He would be called the Son of God.

And in the sixth month the angel Gabriel was sent from God unto a City of Galilee, named Nazareth, to a virgin espoused to a man whose name was Joseph, of the house of David; and the virgin's name was Mary. And the angel came in unto her, and said, Hail, thou that art highly favored, the Lord is with thee: blessed are thou among women. And when she saw him, she was troubled at his sayings, and cast in her mind what manner of salutation is this should be. And the angel said unto her, fear not Mary; for thou hast found favor with God. And, behold thou shalt conceive in thy womb, and bring forth a son and thou shalt call his name JESUS. **St Luke 1:26-31**

Then Mary said unto the angel, How shall this be, seeing I know not a man? And the angel answered and said unto her, The Holy Ghost shall come upon thee, and the power of the highest shall overshadow thee: therefore, also that Holy thing which shall be born of thee shall be called the Son of God. **St. Luke 1:34-36**

Although Mary questioned God, she still believed. Again I say, it is nothing wrong with asking God questions, but when he responds with a Word that does not fit with the normal "status quo" of things in the traditional church, you must challenge yourself to believe Him. Many believers miscarriage their destiny because of unbelief. Mary believed this prophetic Word that she had received from beyond the veil. She immediately arose and went to Elisabeth's house, who was six months pregnant with John. And when Mary entered the house, her mere salutation, caused John to leap in Elisabeth's womb and Elisabeth was filled with the Holy Ghost.

And Mary said, Behold the handmaid of the Lord; be it unto me according thy word. And the angel departed from her. And Mary arose in those days, and went into the hill country with haste, into a city of Judea; and entered into the house of Zechariah, and saluted Elisabeth. And it came to pass, that when Elisabeth heard the salutation of Mary, the babe leaped in her womb; and Elisabeth was filled with the Holy Ghost. **St. Luke 139:41**

So it is in the natural, so it is in the spirit.   Many Believers are six months pregnant with purpose and destiny and are in need of a rhema Word that will activate the seed of God's promise within them...... a Word that will cause the seed to leap in their spiritual womb, just like John leaped inside of Elisabeth. This rhema Word will push you beyond the veil, into the very presence of God.   God's prophetic Word to you is.........."Don't die in the sixth month, of your spiritual growth in him". Don't die praying at the altar of incense, and never enter into His presence, beyond the veil, to experience all God has for you. The trials, the tests, the pain, the hurt, the disappointments, and the many nights of weeping and crying, were all for your spiri-tual growth and maturity. *Your wilderness is your birthing canal.*   Position yourself to hear, believe, receive, and obey every Word that God sends to you from the third dimension of His Glory, from beyond the veil, and get ready to step over into your season of birthing.   Beyond the veil is where your season meets your set time (this will be discussed further in the next chapter).   This is a place, in God, where you are ready to birth all the promises the Lord have for you. But you must be mindful that this is a significant place, in your spiritual growth, where you must remain in divine covenant with believers who are not just going through the motion of church, but have spent time with God to receive revelation and divine impartation from beyond the veil. Consider again that Elisabeth was six months pregnant when Mary went to her house (**St. Luke 1:36**). **St. Luke 1:56** says that Mary remained with Elisabeth for three months......meaning that Mary remained with Elisabeth for the last trimester of her pregnancy, the seventh to the ninth month. Why would Mary consider remaining with Elisabeth for the last three months of her pregnancy? The same reason you need divine covenant relationships, that have been ordained by God to continuously activate the seed of God's promise within you, when you are on the verge of birthing your divine destiny. These are relationships that have been orchestrated by God, and not by man. They are individuals the Lord have preordained, before the foundation of the world, who can connect and understand what God has

41

placed within your spirit. They are individuals who understand rhema Word that comes directly from the Throne of God.

They are individuals who don't think you have jumped off the deep end when you get a revelation that does not add up to the normal status quo of traditional church. Both Mary and Elisabeth had something in common. They were experiencing a spiritual realm in God that could not be explained in the natural. Elisabeth was barren and Mary had never been with a man, but they both were impregnated with a seed of promise. You must be sensitive to the Holy Ghost during this level of your spiritual walk with God, to make sure that you are divinely connected to believers who will activate the seed of God's promise in you, and not individuals who will deactivate the seed, and as a result, you abort your destiny in the third trimester of your spiritual growth. Word to the wise..... *"Divine connection is based upon spirit, not flesh"*.

Chapter Three
When Season Meets Set Time

Through the revelation of God's Word, I was gradually understanding where the Lord was trying to take me. He was trying to get me to a place in Him to birth out every promise He had revealed to me over the years. I was having difficulty connecting all of what I was experiencing with the process of spiritual growth and maturity, even though God had shown me many things about my divine destiny, through years of dreams and visions. I was simply going through the motion of church, and at the same time not having a clue that I was in the birthing canal of the wilderness experience.

The Lord continued to show me things in the scripture that I had never perceived before. I would read a scripture over and over again, and see something even more profound each time I would read it. This went on for years in my life. Then it hit me. God said to me, "the messages I am giving to you, are to you first". Now, most of us who are ministers of the Gospel should know this, but what I was missing was that God was helping me to understand and see my personal level of growth in Him, through the revelation of the Word He was revealing to me. This is how you know you have moved from the second dimension, where you just hear the Word, to the third dimension, beyond the veil, where you apply what you have heard, in the second. It becomes rhema in your life. You began to apply the knowledge you've acquired from every bible study class, Sunday morning messages, and personal study time with God. The messages being given to me by God, were messages that gave me clarity and understanding about my place in Him, at that point in my spiritual growth. I began to see myself in the very messages I delivered to others. Now, most won't admit that while you are preaching on forgiveness, the Lord is telling you that is exactly what you need to do....... *"forgive"*. Most in leadership want to appear as if they always have it together, and they are on their way to heaven. Needless to say, it is more like going through hell, trying to get to heaven..........not realizing you can get stuck in the midst of your hellish experience, receive an impartation from the enemy of your own soul, and miss God. That's what the "beyond the veil" experience is all about. You know when an individual has not been beyond the veil, because they can see everything that is wrong with another, but can never see themselves. It's like living in a "make believe" world that's filled with hypocrisy. <u>Beyond the veil, believers are not quick to judge or be critical.</u> They will give the worse situation the benefit of the doubt. They will see the good, before they see the evil. They can know the enemy is using a vessel to attempt to destroy them, but they will strive to love, and see the good in the midst of all the evil. Think about it..........if God rewarded us for the many times we've failed or missed Him, most of us would not be alive today. But He sees where you are going, not where you are. Whether or not you arrive at that place, depends on you and your obedience to God. We all know that

we don't always deserve the many blessings the Lord give to us, but He blesses us
anyway.   He rains on the just, as well as,
the unjust.   You should stop right now, and
lift your hands and tell God, *"Thank You"*
for extending his grace and mercy at times
when you knew you did not deserve it.
When Jesus died, grace and mercy went
with Him into the Most Holy Place, beyond
the veil, and sat on the throne. That's why
we can go in boldly and ask for help in the
time of need.

> *Let us therefore come boldly unto the*
> *throne of grace, that we may obtain*
> *mercy and find grace to help in the*
> *time of need.* **Hebrews 4:16**

How much grace and mercy, that has been
extended to you, are you willing to give
unto others?   I can still hear the words of
the average believer saying, "I want to be
like Jesus".   "I want to walk like Him, and
talk like Him".   But can you love and forgive like Him?   Once again, there is a price
to be paid.

I must take a moment again to reflect on the book *Spiritual Ejaculation: The Final Hours of Great Deception*. The foundation of this revelation was based on my own personal need to forgive those who had trespassed against me. I had spent many nights sleeping with the spirit of unforgiveness and depression, which I spoke about in this book. God revealed to me that the enemy can release spirits into your life, because of past devastating experiences. We can become intimate with these unclean spirits, and as a result, you can potentially miscarriage the seed of God's Word within you.

After the book was written and published, I was tested in the very content, because I had to forgive those who, first of all, criticized and persecuted me, merely because of the title. God allowed me to live through the very revelation of what He was showing me relative to the first, second and third dimension of spiritual growth and maturity. I began to understand that most believers who are afraid to accept or receive anything from God, that is not common to the traditional religious church in the second dimension, are usually those who have never had a "beyond the veil" experience in the third dimension. They are believers who simply go to church and enjoy the charismatic flow of a religious setting that allow them to be comfortable in a lukewarm state. In other words, they are about to die in the sixth month of spiritual growth. Some are even at the altar of incense praying, like Zechariah, but never have gone beyond the veil, to hear what God is saying in His presence.

I felt myself living every revelation God had ever given me. This was really an eye opening experience. The scripture became more real to me in **St. John 1:12**....... "But as many as received Him, to them He gave power to become the Sons of God". It is a process. The Lord gives us His Spirit, which is the Holy Ghost, to overcome the enemy, but we must obey. If we don't obey, we become bastards and not sons. How many bastards are sitting in the church, who firmly believe that they are Sons of God, just because they came to the altar and gave their life to Jesus, and they spoke in other tongues? You are not a Son of God until you go through the birthing process of being obedient to his Word in every area of your life.

> *For whom God loveth he chasteneth, and scourgeth every son whom he receiveth. If ye endure chastening, God dealeth with you as with sons; for what son is he whom the father chasteneth not? But if ye be without chastisement, whereof all are partakers, then are ye bastards, and not sons.* **Hebrews 12:6-8**

I realized that I was being processed through the birthing canal of the wilderness experience.......having a face to face encounter with the enemy of my own soul. It's like a fetus being developed in the mother's womb for nine months (38-42 weeks). God, my heavenly Father, was developing and nourishing me through the rhema Word He was feeding me from the third dimension. He was beckoning me to come into His presence. I had a choice to accept the call to go in beyond the veil, or miscarriage my destiny in the second dimension, receiving knowledge of Him, but never experiencing the revelation of that knowledge.

As God began to process me through every rhema Word He had given me, I began to see how you can be in a "season" of blessings but have not yet met your "set time". Take a moment and look again at the diagram in chapter two. God revealed to me that your season begins when you make a decision to step beyond the veil and hear all God has to say to "you". This is the place where you long to be in His presence, and you began to cry out for more of God. You are simply tired of the "status quo" of traditional church. Now, I know you have heard me say this several times in this book. Needless to say, many believers who are simply churching would read this book for curiosity and say... "Well, it just don't take all that". Well, I am so glad Jesus did not say that when He died for you on the cross, being whipped and beaten, with blood dripping down His face, with piercing thrones in His head. I am glad He did not look into your future and say, "It's not *worth* all that". I must tell you, the death of Jesus is symbolic to the price you will have to pay to birth your destiny. You too, will go through a spiritual death, burial and resurrection. Paul said, "Always bearing about in the body, the dying of the Lord Jesus, that the life of Jesus might be made manifest in our body". "For we which live are always delivered unto death for Jesus sake, that the life also of Jesus may be made manifest in our mortal flesh" **(II Corinthians 4:10-11)**. What is so frightening is that many desire to be resurrected, but many do not want to will themselves to the death of the cross. And believe it or not, many are being resurrected, but not in the Christ anointing. Many want to be a *"wonder"*, to gain recognition from men. But you will never be a *wonder*, until people wonder where you are. This is the place in your spiritual growth where you have been shoved into the tomb, and it is believed to be all over for you. The enemy actually feels as though his plot to destroy you has succeeded.

I began to look back over my life and see how the Lord had really blessed me in many areas of my life, but I had not yet seen the birthing, or the manifestation of many of the dreams and visions relative to my divine destiny. I realized that you can be walking in a season of blessings and revelation, but still have not yet birthed all the promises the Lord have for your life.

I remember when I was very young in the Lord, I would have dreams and visions about flying......... not on an airplane, but in the spirit. I would actually be flying in my dreams. Many times I would literally be running from the enemy, in an attempt to save my life. Flying was always my way of escape in my dreams. Many times I would awaken in the morning feeling very tired, as though I had really been flying all night long. One night, I had a dream where I was actually flying over the continent of Africa. There were so many people that I could not reach them from the platform. I had to literally fly over the masses of people to be able to minister to all of them, because the multitude of people was so great. I knew that the call of God was upon life for ministry in foreign land. I would always, say to my children, "Do you want to go to Africa with me?" Of course, they were very young at the time, so they really thought their mother had lost it. But these words would just utter out of my mouth from within, as if someone, somewhere was calling me to Africa. I was constantly getting prophecies about being called to foreign land, particularly Africa. Ministry in Africa was my dream, and my heart's desire. It was not only a dream, but it was divine destiny. So for more than twelve years of my saved life, I had many nights of dreams and visions of flying and ministering in Africa. Suddenly, about seven years ago, I stopped having these dreams and the visions, and I asked God........ "Why?" He said to me, "You are not having the dreams or visions anymore, because you have entered into that season of destiny". As I began to reflect upon what the Lord said to me, I realized that it was around 1995 when I stopped having the dreams and visions about Africa. This was the year that I first sat my feet on foreign soil to minister the Word of God in London, England. Although, I had entered into the season of ministry in foreign land, I had not yet birthed my divine destiny of ministry in Africa. My season had not yet met my set time. I began to understand that I had entered into the last trimester, for the birthing of divine destiny, symbolic to the last trimester in natural birth (the seventh to the ninth month).

Refer again to the diagram, and let's consider the natural birth process of a baby during the third trimester (seventh to ninth month). As I've mentioned before, a baby can be born in the seventh month and live, but the baby did not go the full term of nine months. From a spiritual perspective, you can enter into a season where you begin to see God bring to pass some of the promises in your life, but you have not yet met your divine appointment with destiny. I knew that ministry in Africa was a divine appointment with destiny, not London, England. Ministry in London, in 1995, was symbolic to entering into the seventh month of pregnancy, but full term was ministry in Africa. This was a place beyond veil where "season" was getting ready to meet "set time".

While attending a conference in Atlanta, Georgia in June of 2001, Dr. Leona weeks and I began to share and discuss the passion of father and son relationships, in the Body of Christ. I did not know at the time that God had been speaking to Bishop Thomas Wesley Weeks Sr., her husband, about this same need in the Body of Christ. Dr. Leona Weeks began to share with me the vision of New Destiny Fellowship International and invited me to attend the very first meeting, which was being held in Wilmington, Delaware in July of 2001. After my husband and I prayed and consulted the heart of God for direction, we decided at the last minute to drive and take the entire family to Wilmington, Delaware. This was an eighteen hour drive from Pensacola, but we were determined and led of God to attend. It sounded like something we had been looking for, for years. The enemy really did not want us to get to this meeting, because by the time we got to Atlanta our van ran hot. When we stopped to check the van, there was no radiator cap on the radiator. It was evident that the mechanic, who serviced the van prior to our leaving Pensacola, had left the radiator cap completely off or lose, and all the water evaporated out of the radiator. As a result, the motor in our van was destroyed. But we did not allow this to stop us. We simply left the car in Atlanta to be repaired, rented another vehicle, and kept going. I shared that, because many times we get very close to the divine Will of God for our lives, and when difficult times arise, we end up aborting our blessing.

We had been faithfully committed to the Pentecostal Assemblies of the World for several years of the pastorate, until God began to lead us differently. For some time, we had been searching the heart of God for the proper covering, since our separation from this covering. Let me take a moment here and say to you how important it is for you to be divinely covered by the spiritual parent, who has been assigned to you by God. Consider again naturally, a baby cannot be born unless the seed of the man is released into the womb of the woman. So it is spiritually. Your destiny cannot be born, until you are divinely connected to the spiritual parent, who has your seed of destiny, locked inside of their vision. This seed of destiny can only be released into your life, through divine obedience to God.

So although we had to drive eighteen hours, we were compelled by God to attend this first meeting, which was the birthing of New Destiny Fellowship International. At the meeting, my husband and I immediately knew that this was the Will of God for us, and for the ministry the Lord had afforded us to pastor, in Pensacola, for the past twelve years. We were very moved by the level of organization and the clear well defined direction of the visionary Bishop Thomas Wesley Weeks, Sr.. Needless to say, I had no idea, at the time, that God was positioning me to fulfill my divine appointment with destiny in Africa.

In November, 2002, my "season" finally met my "set time" when I went to minister in Ghana, West Africa, with Bishop Thomas Wesley Sr. and a crusade team of about twenty people. It was an experience that will forever be marked in my spirit. I really began to understand the totality of the things I had to encounter to get to this place of purpose. I could clearly see, after ministering in Africa, that there is a level of warfare in that country that can only be conquered through total obedience to the death, burial and resurrection process of spiritual growth and maturity.

Consider some food for thought. You were not born in your own womb. Your mother had to carry you for nine months. Therefore, you cannot spiritually birth yourself into destiny without submission to the vessel who has been assigned to escort you into destiny. Most of those who are seeking to "arrive", without paying a price, would frown upon this statement, because many individuals in the church don't want to submit to anything or anybody. There is a spirit of rebellion that is running like wild in the Body of Christ. Sad to say, the enemy has fooled many to believe that their rebellion against leadership is the Will of God. So they hop from church to church, receiving even greater levels of rebellion each time they make a move outside the Will of God.

Ministry in Africa was a vision of Bishop Thomas Wesley Weeks, Sr. This vision had my divine appointment with Africa locked inside of it. It was through my husband and I's obedience to God that caused the seed of destiny to be birthed in my life. Your seed of destiny is awaiting you.... to be unlocked, through total obedience and submission to God's Will for your life.........then and only then will your "season" meet your "set time". Your set time is the place in your life where you finally meet the "real you" who God spoke about before you were born...........like He did Jeremiah. It is the place in your life, where your true identity and purpose for being born is finally released into the earth realm.

Chapter Four
Resurrected In A New Identity

I cannot explain how fulfilled I felt the night I ministered for the first time in Africa, in November of 2002. It was almost as though I had been there before. I knew that I had stepped over into divine destiny for this season in my life. I was so overwhelmed by the presence of God. The manifestation of many years of dreams, visions and prophecies were flashing before my eyes, causing me to be very broken before the Lord. It was a moment in my life when titles, earthly accomplishments and possessions were literally stripped from my consciousness. It did not matter. I was in a place where God had ordained me to be before I was even formed in my mother's womb. I had met the "real me", who could not be identified by the name of Dr. Janice Crenshaw. It was an experience that could not be summed up in an earthly title, or earthly resume.

Every believer must realize that there is an identity that has been given to you that can only be unveiled, from beyond the veil. You must strive to enter into that place in God to discover who you were pre-destined to be. Remember Jacob who wrestled with the presence of God all night long, so much so that the Lord revealed that his true identity was Israel, and his name would no longer be Jacob.

> *And Jacob was left alone; and there wrestled a man with him until the breaking of the day. And when he saw that he prevailed not against him, he touched the hollow of his thigh; and the hollow of Jacob's thigh was out of joint, as he wrestled with him. And he said, let me go, for the day breaketh. And he said, I will not let thee go, except thou bless me. And he said unto him, What is thy name? And he said Jacob. And he said, thy name shall be called no more Jacob, but Israel: for as a prince thou hast power with God and man, and hast prevailed.*
> **Genesis 32:24-28**

Are you willing to wrestle your way through the wilderness experiences of life, when all hell has broken lose and everything is out of place, like Jacob's joint was out of place........ to get the release of your true identity in God? It requires a willingness to submit to the death, burial and resurrection process of spiritual growth.

Consider the diagram again. Notice that the position of nine months (forty weeks of pregnancy), relative to natural pregnancy, is symbolic to the conclusion of the forty year wilderness experience. The Lord revealed to me that you will go through some trying times in your life before you birth your divine destiny. True destiny is birthed in the very presence of God. You will never know your real purpose for being born, unless you strive to enter into His presence. Let me clarify...... this revelation has nothing to do with the exact number of years, months or even weeks you may experience dry seasons in your life, but it does indicate that the length of time it takes you to go through the birthing canal of wilderness experiences, is dependant upon your total obedience to God.

Just like the children of Israel who could
have made their journey through the wilderness into Canaan in a few days, they
wondered for forty years, because of disobedience.   The key is....... "don't die in
the wilderness".   Many believers get frus-
trated, even to the point of natural and
spiritual suicide------the same suicide spirit
that was in the midst of the wilderness in
St. Matthew the 4th chapter.   In St. Matthew 4:6 , the devil took Jesus up to the
holy city and sat him on a pinnacle of the
temple and said, "If thou be the Son of
God, cast thyself down: for it is written,
He shall give His angels charge over thee".
Satan attempted to use the Word of God to
persuade Jesus to commit an act of suicide.
This is the same thing the devil does when
you are in the midst of a dry season in your
life....going through a wilderness experience, on your way to your divine destiny.
He will use the knowledge that you have of
God's Word to try and get you to destroy
your own life.   That's why you need more
than just a logos Word (the written Word).
You need a rhema Word that gives you
revelation.......it brings life to you, in the
midst of your trouble.   But you   have a

choice to make the wilderness a place of praise, or a place of murmuring and complaining, like the children of Israel did when the Lord brought them out of Egypt. Every believer has the authority to change the atmosphere of their own wilderness experience by their obedience to God.

Don't bow down to the glory of the enemy in the midst of your wilderness experience.

Don't bow down to the enemy in the midst of your wilderness experience, trying to get a quick transfer into the blessed land. In other words, don't abort your destiny trying to avoid the death, burial and resurrection process.......meaning you will do anything to keep from being persecuted or being displayed on the cross, even if it means persecuting others, lying and cheating to secure personal success.

To get to the next level in God, you are going to be killed. You're simply not going to die of natural causes......... you will be set up and killed, and most times by the religious crowd. Jesus was set up to die by the religious crowd. He knew he had to go to Jerusalem to be killed by the scribes and the Chief priests.

> *From that time forth began Jesus to show unto his disciples, how that he must go unto Jerusalem, and suffer many things of the elders and chief priests and Scribes, and be **killed**, and be raised again the third day.*
> **St. Matthew 16:21**

That same killing spirit is still in the earth today. The religious crowd knows the letter of the Word (second dimension), but have no spiritual insight into the revelation of God's Word (third dimension). You too must willingly go to your "Jerusalem" ...... *the place* where you know that you are being sent, by God, to be killed for His name sake. This is the true test of obedience. How many of us are willing to take our flesh into a situation where we know we are being set up to be crucified? Most believers try to avoid pain, suffering and persecution. Most of us want to be liked and loved by everybody, whether they be saint or sinner. Well, you will never get to the place of a new identity in Christ, being resurrected in a place of true destiny and purpose, unless you will your flesh to be *set -up* for death.

There is a significant difference between just *dying* and *being killed*. Jesus could have simply died of a heart attack, cancer, or just slept away........he's God. He had the authority to lay his life down, but He willed Himself to be set up for *"killing"*. As a matter of fact, Jesus could have given up His life in the wilderness when the devil took Him up to the pinnacle of the temple, and been resurrected after an act of suicide......He holds the power of life and death in His hands. But that was not the plan of God. From a spiritual perspective that would have given the spirit of suicide the right to have dominion in the wilderness. Meaning, if Jesus had submitted to the devil's strategy, the spirit of suicide would have the authority to overtake us, when we go through wilderness experiences in our lives. But Jesus took authority over that spirit, and because of that, now every believer has that same authority.

Needless to say, many are committing spiritual suicide in the wilderness by bowing down to the enemy during spiritually dry seasons in their lives.

The third level of glory is resurrection

Where there's a death---- there's truly a resurrection. But every resurrection does not have power. In other words, if you submit to Satan in the midst of your wilderness experience, and commit spiritual suicide, you too will have a day of resurrection, but you will not be resurrected in the Christ anointing.   Food   for   thought.........how many people have been resurrected due to a suicidal death in the wilderness, and not from being *killed* on the cross?   This means they were illegally transferred to the second level of glory *"the tomb"*.   They chose to skip the true death of the cross in hopes of getting through the wilderness experience without being totally obedient to God. This is what you call an illegal resurrection--- that grants an illegal entry into the blessed land. Why do you think the devil said to Jesus that he would give Him all the kingdoms of this world in a moment's time, if He would bow down and worship him? (**St. Matthew 4: 8-9**). Satan will offer you a quick fix to receive a counterfeit blessing that is only temporal, and not eternal. These blessings are not only counterfeit, but the anointing is counterfeit, as well.

Remember in the book of Judges the 3rd chapter, the Lord spoke to the children to Israel and told them that he left some nations there to prove them, because they knew not the wars of Canaan.

Now these are the nations that the Lord left to prove Israel by them, even as many of Israel as had not known all the wars of Canaan; only that the generations of the Children of Israel might know, to teach them war, at the least such as before knew nothing thereof. Namely, five lords of the Philistines, and all the Canaanites, and the Sidonians, and the Hivites, that dwelt in mount Lebanon, from mount Baalhermon

> *unto the entering in of Hamath. And they were to prove Israel by them, to know whether they would hearken unto the commandments of the Lord, which he commanded their fathers by the hand of Moses.* **Judges 3:1-4**

Let's look at this scripture prophetically. The Lord specifically said that he left these nations there to prove Israel by them. Meaning the Lord has left some wilderness experiences in your life to prove you before you get to your blessed place of promise. If you are not proven, you can get into your blessed place of promise and still abort your destiny. You must be aware that inside of this wilderness are enemies that have been assigned to attack you. The enemy is not always from without, but many times from within. God is trying to get the Amorite, the Jebusite and the Canaanite out of you before you get to your blessed land. The danger here is to not allow yourself to become intimate with the very thing that God has left in the midst of your wilderness experience to prove you. God never intended for you to be intimate with your wilderness experience, nor the enemy in your wilderness. That means God does not want you to give more attention to the wilderness experiences in your life, than you give to praising and worshiping Him in the wilderness. That's why Jesus went back to the wilderness immediately after he received the Holy Ghost to destroy the influence of Satan in this spiritual place. We must see the wilderness from a spiritual perspective......beyond seeing it in the natural as being a place where there's no water, no trees, and dry land. The wilderness is a spiritual place for every believer..........a place where you are tested and tried by the enemy, and you sometimes want to give up. *It is your birthing canal.* If you've never had wilderness experiences, as a believer, then one would have to question if you have truly taken on the life of Jesus.

> *Always bearing about in the body the dying of the Lord Jesus, that the life also of Jesus might be made manifest in our body. For we which live are always delivered unto death for Jesus' sake, that the life also of Jesus might be made manifest in our mortal flesh.* **II Corinthians 4:10-11**

Your new identity in Christ, being resurrected into divine purpose and destiny, can only be accomplished through your willingness to go through the death, burial and resurrection process of spiritual growth and maturity. The wilderness experience is a part of this process. Wilderness experiences are not continuously repetitious, but these experiences do enhance your maturity in God. Many are struggling to find their identity through association, instead of allowing God to prepare them for a resurrection. So they spend a lot of time trying to fit into the religious click of an identity that will be acceptable to man, instead of allowing God to take them through the process to birth their divine destiny. Let me put it more bluntly...... "there is a danger is trying to discover destiny by association, rather than a Christ-like resurrection".

There is a danger in trying to discover destiny by association, Rather than a Christ-like resurrection.

It reminds me when the Lord spoke to me about coming forth out of the tomb.

It was a time in my life where I was literally trying to find spiritual relationships inside of a dead place......a place where God had called me out of. The spirit of loneliness and depression had almost overtaken me. One day the Lord literally spoke to me and said, "You are lonely because you choose to stay in the tomb, when I have called you to another level in me". "I have called you to resurrection". The Lord continued to minister to me. He said, " my child, no one is going to respond to you in the tomb"....they can't hear you." "Why do you keep knocking on tomb stones, waiting for a response?" He said it again, "Stop trying to find relationships in the tomb". What the Lord was saying to me was that there were many church going people in the tomb, who had been transferred to the tomb, by committing spiritual suicide in the wilderness, and not because they had passed the test of public display on the cross. Some were church going people who had aborted their destiny in the wilderness experience, by bowing down to Satan...... trying to get a quick transfer into the blessed land. The Lord said to me, "Therefore, when you need a listening ear, someone to talk to, you find can no one ...because you are looking in the wrong place.... "the tomb". "They can't feel what you feel, neither can they see what you see". "They can only condemn you, not comfort you, because they have not paid the price". Let me stop here, because even as I write, the Holy Ghost speaks to me.............I want to clarify that this revelation does not mean that God perceives you as being better than any other believer in Christ, when He is moving you from one spiritual level to the next, because He has no respect of persons. It simply means that you need to know where you stand in your relationship with God, and you can only understand where you are in God, by receiving revelation that comes from a divine impartation that's on the same level that God has moved you into. In other words, you may be in a low place, but God is sending you a Word that is on a higher level.........the level He is calling you to. The strong must bear the infirmities of the weak......the weak can't bear the infirmities of the weak (**Romans 15:1**). Let me try to explain this further. In **St. Luke 1:57**, when Elisabeth birthed John, her neighbors and family wanted to name the child Zechariah, and Elisabeth said, "not so, his name is John". I would have to wonder how did Elisabeth get this information. The angel Gabriel came to Zechariah while he was praying at the altar of incense, not Elisabeth...... to tell him that Elisabeth was going to have a child and his name would be John. It would seem evident to me that this revelation had to be revealed to Elisabeth after she received the Holy Ghost, when Mary came to her house and saluted her. First of all, Zechariah had not spoken since the Lord shut his mouth, because he did not believe that Elisabeth was going to have a child. Elisabeth's neighbors and family were ready to label John with an earthly identity that did not belong to him. He was not Zachariah Jr.......he was John. But because Elisabeth had received a divine impartation that had nothing to do with information she had received from the earth realm, she immediately declared that the child's name was John. I can just imagine how Zechariah felt listening to this conversation, and not being able to speak, knowing that he had been told nine months ago that Elisabeth would have a child and his name would be John. Family and neighbors were looking to Zechariah to disagree with Elisabeth, wondering how could he just sit there and not agree to name the child Zechariah Jr.. Grant it no one in the family was named John. So to affirm that Elisabeth had heard from the Lord, Zechariah asked for a writing pad and began to write on a tablet............"his name is John"...and immediately his tongue was loosed and Zechariah was able to speak again.

> *Now when Elisabeths' full time came that she should be delivered; and she brought forth a son. And her neighbors and her cousins heard how the Lord showed great mercy upon her; and they rejoiced with her. And it came to pass, that on the eighth day they came to circumcise the child; and they called him Zechariah, after the name of his father. And the mother answered and said, not so, but he shall be called John. And they said unto her, there is none of thy kindred that is called by this name. And they made signs to his*

father, how he would have him called, and he asked for a writing table, and wrote, saying, his name is John. And they marveled all. And his mouth was opened immediately, and his tongue loosed, and he spake, and praised God. **St. Luke 1:57-64**

I would have to ask....... "How many be-lievers have received earthly identities that have not been ordained by God, because of association and not resurrection?" By asso-ciation, Zechariah was John's earthly fa-ther, but Zechariah Jr. was not his name. I challenge you to find out who you were purposed to be in this life. If you don't seek God and allow yourself to go through the birthing process....society, and those who are going through the motion of tradi-tional church will label your identity....and it may not be the identity the Lord has pre-destined for you.

This revelation brought me ultimate peace to understanding my personal rela-tionship with God, and every level of growth the Lord had taken me through, and is still taking me through to become a true

Son of God. I realized that I had spent months, and maybe even years missing the call of God to another level in Him, because I did not understand the death, burial, and resurrection process for spiritual growth and maturity. I almost aborted my destiny going to church, receiving prophecies that were not coming from the third dimension, and trying to get validation from those who had received illegal resurrections and transfers into Canaan (the blessed land), without paying the price. I am *grateful* (the title of my new CD) to God that he caught me in time, before I aborted my destiny in the midst of my wilderness experience.

There is a new identity awaiting you to be revealed from beyond the veil. Stay committed to the process, shown on the next page, and you will *legally* possess all the promises the Lord have for you.

Spiritual Growth & Maturity

LEVELS OF GLORY	LIKENESS OF JESUS	NATURE OF MAN
1st Level: The Cross Public Display	**Death: Outer Court** (Brazen Altar)	**Body**
2nd Level: The Tomb The Dark & Lonely Place	**Burial: Inner Court** (Holy Place)	**Soul**
3rd Level: Resurrection Place of Divine Destiny	**Resurrection: Beyond The Veil** (Most Holy Place)	**Spirit**

In my conclusion, you must stay on the brazen altar (the Outer Court) long enough for God to burn off the desires of the flesh. The Holy place (the Inner Court) is where you are taught the Word of God, and you allow yourself to be buried in the knowledge of His Word. Needless to say, consider how many believers are buried in *head knowledge* of God's Word, but have never experienced being resurrected to another level in God? To be buried......is to be resurrected. Otherwise, you eventually die from simply going to church---- continuously getting information, and never receiving revelation that is available to you from beyond the veil. You must be forever mindful that your *flesh* is your greatest enemy. The brazen altar (Outer Court) is not a very comfortable place. Most would rather skip over this process of growth and jump on over into the inner court (the Holy Place), and just go through the charismatic flow of traditional church....never experiencing true repentance. Be reminded that this is exactly what the enemy wants ...... he wants you to miscarriage your destiny, in the sixth month's right before you break beyond the veil (refer again to the diagram in chapter two). In the inner court (the Holy Place), there's a constant battle in the mind or *soul*---- warfare between the flesh and the spirit. The enemy wants you to just be a hearer of the Word and not a doer. This is the level, in your spiritual growth, where you will have the tendency to backslide.... sitting right in the church every Sunday hearing message after message. One day you want to be saved, and the next day you are not sure. Beyond the veil is where the *spirit* is in control, and you are *resurrected* in the likeness of Jesus Christ. You've learned how to overcome the battle of the mind, and submit to the Spirit of God and His Will for your life. This is the level of growth where you meet your divine destiny. You finally become acquainted with the *"You"* ....the person that God predestined before the foundation of the world. It is then....at this place of spiritual maturity that the revelation of the words of Paul finally become a reality in your life....that I may know Him, in the power of His resurrection, and in the fellowship of His suffering, being made conformable unto His death. (**Philippians 3:10**)

Apply this revelatory Word to your life and get ready to step over into your divine destiny.

A WORD OF WISDOM

The revelation and the natural principles that have been shared with you in this book are in no way to indicate to you that you will have to experience any set number of years, weeks or even days, of wilderness experiences before you walk into your season of destiny. What God is saying, is that you will have wilderness experiences in your life, but you don't have to spend forty years or even forty days in a dry wilderness place in your life, trying to find your way to purpose. It all depends upon your total obedience to God, and faith in His Word. God can, and God will redeem the time you have lost, just going through the motion of traditional church. These applied principles are simply a way to help you understand that there is order in everything that God does........so it is in the natural, so it is in the spirit, because He made all things after the counsel of His own Will.

Other published works by the Author:

Books:

Inspirational Readings on Victorious Living

**Spiritual Ejaculation:
The Final Hours Of Great Deception**

Gospel Music CD:

Jesus Lifted Me

Grateful

To Order you may log onto
www.drjanicecrenshaw.com
or
Call (850) 439-0022